Giving
God
Your
Best

EXCELLENT LIVING

Interactions Small Group Series

Authenticity: Being Honest with God and Others
Big Questions: Clear Answers to Confusing Issues
Celebrating God: Discover the Truth of God's Character
Character: Reclaiming Six Endangered Qualities
Commitment: Developing Deeper Devotion to Christ
Community: Building Relationships within God's Family
Essential Christianity: Practical Steps for Spiritual Growth
Excellent Living: Giving God Your Best
Fruit of the Spirit: Living the Supernatural Life
Getting a Grip: Finding Balance in Your Daily Life
Influence: Maximizing Your Impact for God
Jesus: Seeing Him More Clearly
Lessons on Love: Building Deeper Relationships
Living in God's Power: Finding God's Strength for Life's Challenges
Love in Action: Experiencing the Joy of Serving
Marriage: Building Real Intimacy
Meeting God: Psalms for the Highs and Lows of Life
New Identity: Discovering Who You Are in Christ
Parenting: How to Raise Spiritually Healthy Kids
Prayer: Opening Your Heart to God
Reaching Out: Sharing God's Love Naturally
The Real Deal: Discover the Rewards of Authentic Relationships
Significance: Understanding God's Purpose for Your Life
Transformation: Letting God Change You from the Inside Out

InterActions
small group series

Giving
God
Your
Best

EXCELLENT
LIVING

BILL HYBELS
WITH KEVIN AND SHERRY HARNEY

ZONDERVAN®

WILLOW
Willow Creek Resources

ZONDERVAN.com/
AUTHORTRACKER
follow your favorite authors

ZONDERVAN

Excellent Living
Copyright © 2010 by Willow Creek Association

Requests for information should be addressed to:

Zondervan, *Grand Rapids, Michigan 49530*

ISBN 978-0-310-28064-4

Interior design by Rick Devon and Michelle Espinoza

Printed in the United States of America

09 10 11 12 13 14 15 16 17 18 • 20 19 18 17 16 15 14 13 12 11 10 9 8 7 6 5 4 3 2 1

CONTENTS

INTERACTIONS

In 1992, Willow Creek Community Church, in partnership with Zondervan and the Willow Creek Association, released a curriculum for small groups entitled the Walking with God series. In just three years, almost a half million copies of these small group study guides were being used in churches around the world. The phenomenal response to this curriculum affirmed the need for relevant and biblical small group materials.

At the writing of this curriculum, there were nearly 3,000 small groups meeting regularly within the structure of Willow Creek Community Church. We believe this number will increase as we continue to place a central value on small groups. Many other churches throughout the world are growing in their commitment to small group ministries as well, so the need for resources is increasing.

In response to this great need, the Interactions small group series has been developed. Willow Creek Association and Zondervan have joined together to create a whole new approach to small group materials. These discussion guides are meant to challenge group members to a deeper level of sharing, create lines of accountability, move followers of Christ into action, and help group members become fully devoted followers of Christ.

SUGGESTIONS FOR INDIVIDUAL STUDY

1. Begin each session with prayer. Ask God to help you understand the passage and to apply it to your life.
2. A good modern translation, such as the New International Version, Today's New International Version, the New American Standard Bible, or the New Revised Standard Version, will give you the most help. Questions in this guide are based on the New International Version.
3. Read and reread the passage(s). You must know what the passage says before you can understand what it means and how it applies to you.
4. Write your answers in the spaces provided in the study guide. This will help you to express clearly your understanding of the passage.
5. Keep a Bible dictionary handy. Use it to look up unfamiliar words, names, or places.

Suggestions for Group Study

1. Come to the session prepared. Careful preparation will greatly enrich your time in group discussion.
2. Be willing to join in the discussion. The leader of the group will not be lecturing but will encourage people to discuss what they have learned in the passage. Plan to share what God has taught you in your individual study.
3. Stick to the passage being studied. Base your answers on the verses being discussed rather than on outside authorities such as commentaries or your favorite author or speaker.
4. Try to be sensitive to the other members of the group. Listen attentively when they speak, and be affirming whenever you can. This will encourage more hesitant members of the group to participate.
5. Be careful not to dominate the discussion. By all means participate, but allow others to have equal time.
6. If you are the discussion leader, you will find additional suggestions and helpful ideas in the Leader's Notes.

Additional Resources and Teaching Materials

At the end of this study guide you will find a collection of resources and teaching materials to help you in your growth as a follower of Christ. You will also find resources that will help your church develop and build fully devoted followers of Christ.

Introduction:
Giving God
Your Best

Some words have fallen out of use and popularity in modern vocabulary. A number of them show up in this one verse written by the apostle Paul over two thousand years ago:

Finally, brothers, whatever is true, whatever is noble, whatever is right, whatever is pure, whatever is lovely, whatever is admirable — if anything is excellent or praiseworthy — think about such things. (Phil. 4:8)

Think about these eight words: *true, noble, right, pure, lovely, admirable, excellent,* and *praiseworthy.* God says through the apostle Paul that we are to "think about such things," to meditate on them so they can shape our lives, impact our relationships, deepen our faith, and mold our future.

In this small group series we will follow Paul's counsel and think about excellence. In a day and age when excellence is often replaced with "good enough" or confused with perfectionism, we will listen for the voice of the Holy Spirit calling us to become the people God longs for us to be. This will mean investigating every part of our lives and seeing ourselves through the lenses of God's pure eyes. It will mean dreaming about a future that will be shaped by His holy hands.

Our example of excellent living is always Jesus. He lived the most excellent life in human history. Radical obedience, sacrificial loving, moral purity, relational intimacy, and so much more marked His life. Jesus loved us with excellence. He never held back. He lived with such commitment to us that it led Him to a cross.

And when it came time for Him to pay the price for sins, Jesus died an excellent death. He carried His own cross. He forgave those who pounded spikes into His hands and feet. He cared for His mother while suffering torment. Within moments of His final breath, He made room for a repentant thief to enter heaven. He cried out, "It is finished," as our sins were covered by His blood.

After His resurrection and ascension, Jesus launched an excellent and dynamic organism called the church. This body of people would express His love to the world throughout the generations. He called us to an excellent mission. He is preparing an excellent eternity for all of us who put our faith and trust in Him.

Now we are called to follow the Savior. Every area of life can reflect excellence as we seek to be like the One who lived and died for us. In this small group study we will look at six distinct aspects of life that can be lived with excellence:

- Our *spiritual* lives,
- Our *moral* lives,
- Our *relational* lives,
- Our *financial* lives,
- The *directional* aspect of our lives,
- And our *eternal* lives.

In a world where "mediocrity" is embraced and "good" is praised, it is time for God's people to seek "excellence" for the glory of God.

LIVING
EXCELLENT
SPIRITUAL
LIVES

THE BIG PICTURE

From the beginning of the Bible, God called people to worship Him with excellence. This was reflected in the kinds of offerings they brought to worship — ranging from a pile of grain to an animal sacrifice. It might be hard for people today to understand the religious system of the Old Testament; it may even seem primitive and brutal to us. But God actually commanded His followers to bring offerings that at times included a sacrificial lamb.

God had told His people that whenever it was time for them to bring a lamb to the temple as a worship offering, they should walk through their herds and find the very best one — the blue-ribbon lamb that would bring the most money at the market. This was God's way of saying, "Make an excellent worship offering to me."

Part of the reason God wanted them to bring their best lamb was because hundreds of years later, Jesus Christ would come into the world as His lamb to take away our sins. God knew He was going to give His most excellent lamb for us. So early on in biblical history God foreshadowed this reality by calling people to give their best lamb for Him.

The message was simple: *Bring me your best because I am giving you my best.*

Sadly, with time, the people stopped giving their best offerings and worship. Instead, they began to give their leftovers, whatever was convenient. Instead of people searching their flocks to identify the very best lamb to bring to the temple, they did precisely the opposite. When sacrifice time came, they would begrudgingly walk around their flock looking for a lamb that was blind, or crippled, or leaning against a fence post about ready to keel over and die. Then they would say, "Well, there's one that we don't need. It won't bring any money at the market. I've found my sacrifice."

Does this sound at all familiar? Of course, we don't bring lambs to church with us as offerings anymore. But we can be tempted to toss God our leftovers, to give Him what is convenient. It might look different in our day and age, but the same patterns and temptations remain.

A WIDE ANGLE VIEW

1   What are some of the ways we can be tempted to give our second best (or even our leftovers) when it comes to how we worship and follow God?

- In our offerings

- In our singing

- In our attentiveness in worship services

- In our time

- In the surrender of our heart

- In our service to others

Read Malachi 1:6–14

2 What do you learn about the heart and character of God in this passage?

How does God's character connect to the kind of worship and offerings we should bring Him?

3 What do you learn about the attitudes and motives of God's people in the days of Malachi?

How do you see these attitudes alive in the church today?

How do you see these attitudes at work in your own heart?

SHARPENING THE FOCUS

Read Snapshot "Your Best Commitment"

YOUR BEST COMMITMENT

Few other passages in the Bible have rocked my world as much as this first chapter of Malachi. The prophetic picture of the worthiness of God is staggering. In the light of His glory, we are called to live excellent spiritual lives. One way we do this is by making a wholehearted commitment to God. This means shifting from living with a conditional commitment to an unconditional commitment in our devotion to Jesus Christ.

When this passage first gripped my heart I had never made an unconditional commitment to anything or anyone. I was an "options" guy, an "escape hatch" guy. I was now at a crossroads. It felt like God was calling His people to be totally sold out and surrendered to Him.

What's an appropriate commitment to someone who stopped at nothing, who paid the ultimate price in His commitment to me? I decided if I was going to maintain any degree of personal integrity I had to make a carte blanche commitment to God. Anything short of that would make a mockery of what He did for me. So, trembling, I said, "God, I formally take the limits and the conditions off my commitment to You. I'll do Your bidding, whatever it is. I'll obey Your will and Your ways. I'll go where You ask me to go. I'll say yes to the promptings of Your Spirit, as I understand them. I'll live out this unconditional commitment even if it costs me everything."

I sincerely offered Him the totality of my life. Instead of feeling a sense of disappointment or regret, I felt exactly the opposite ... a surge of spiritual adrenaline. I felt a God-guided adventure coming on. In a curious kind of way, I felt liberated from a self-led, self-limiting life.

4 What has God done to show His commitment to you? (Linger on this question. There will be a few clear answers, but dig deeper in your memory and the Bible and make a good list of the different ways God has revealed and proven His commitment to you.)

5 All of us can be tempted to place conditions and limits on our commitment to God. In our hearts we say, "God, I will do anything, except—" What are some of these limits we can be tempted to place on our devotion to God?

How might our lives change if we truly followed God without reservation and limits?

Read Snapshot "Your Best Affection"

YOUR BEST AFFECTION

Another dimension in our response to this first chapter of Malachi is realizing that God deserves a more sincere form of affection from His children. He deserves a carte blanche commitment . . . absolutely! He also deserves our best affection. He has loved us with unbounded and unreserved passion. In response, we are called to love Him with all our heart, soul, mind, and strength (Mark 12:30).

When this truth struck me, it was uncharted water. I didn't grow up in a family where affection was expressed freely. I was a novice in giving and receiving love. But I discovered through this text, and many others, that God loved me without reservation. His was an excellent love, a costly love, a self-giving, altruistic, well-meaning, heartfelt affection. I had to grapple with how I would respond to this kind of love.

When we begin to grasp the greatness of God's love, we are moved to give Him our best affection. This can take us out of our comfort zone. It could mean making experimental efforts at expressing love to God. It can lead us to adventures of praise and worship we had never imagined before.

---

6 Tell about a time when you were amazed and overwhelmed by the sheer depth and reality of God's love for you. How did you respond to this growing awareness?

7 Think deeply about God's love for you. Then dig deep, get creative, even a little risky, and identify some substantial ways you can respond back. What are some ways we can express our love and praise to God?

What is one expression of love that might stretch you and grow you as a follower of Jesus? What is standing in the way of you expressing your love this way?

Read Snapshot "The Best Contributions of Your Skills and Talents"

THE BEST CONTRIBUTIONS OF YOUR SKILLS AND TALENTS

When God has our best commitment and when our hearts are devoted to Him in love, everything else seems to follow. As we walk closely with Him we find ourselves offering all we have and are to His causes, His vision, and His mission.

Years ago, when this first chapter of Malachi was getting into my soul, it also began to disrupt my life . . . in a big way. I was on the fast track to a career in business. I was only twenty-three years old and barely needed to shave! I had my whole life mapped out. But God was calling me to something else. I actually checked into a hotel and wrestled with God . . . it is all recorded in my personal journal from 1975. Four days later, I took my life, my skills, and my abilities (that I thought were insufficient for the task) and surrendered them all to God.

Part of spiritual excellence is offering back to God all He has given us. This includes our abilities. Even when we feel weak and ill-equipped, God can do amazing things through a willing life.

8

What are some of the unique skills, gifts, and abilities God has given to you?

How are you using one of these for God's glory in:

• Your home?

• The church?

• Your community?

9

What is one gift or ability you have still not offered back to God and leveraged for His purposes in this world?

What step can you take to offer this to God and begin a process of discovering how He can use it for His glory?

PUTTING YOURSELF IN THE PICTURE

Commit It to Memory

A couple of passages from the book of Philippians can help propel you forward as you are learning to live an excellent spiritual life. Read and meditate on these texts. Also, try to memorize one of them and carry it in your heart in the coming days:

But whatever was to my profit I now consider loss for the sake of Christ. What is more, I consider everything a loss compared to the surpassing greatness of knowing Christ Jesus my Lord, for whose sake I have lost all things. I consider them rubbish, that I may gain Christ. (Phil. 3:7–8)

Finally, brothers, whatever is true, whatever is noble, whatever is right, whatever is pure, whatever is lovely, whatever is admirable — if anything is excellent or praiseworthy — think about such things. (Phil. 4:8)

Your Best for His Best

In the coming week, prayerfully reflect on what kind of sacrifice and offering you are giving God. Address only one area a day and use the space below to journal your thoughts. As you consider each area, ask yourself these three questions:

First: Read Malachi 1:6–14 again

1. How excellent is my offering to God in this area?
2. What is God asking of me?
3. What adjustments can I make to surrender more fully to God?

Area of Focus: My offering of time ...

Area of Focus: My offering of finances (both tithe and offerings) ...

Area of Focus: My offering of worship in song ...

Area of Focus: My offering of expressions of love to God ...

Area of Focus: My offering of my gifts and abilities ...

LIVING EXCELLENT MORAL LIVES

REFLECTIONS FROM SESSION 1

1. If you took time to meditate on or memorize Philippians 3:7 – 8 and 4:8, tell your group about what God is teaching you through these passages.
2. Name one way you have been seeking to give God a more pure and acceptable offering since the last time your group met.

THE BIG PICTURE

Does it really pay to live a morally excellent life in a world like ours? Psalm 1 says it does!

Blessed is the man
  who does not walk in the counsel of the wicked
or stand in the way of sinners
  or sit in the seat of mockers.
But his delight is in the law of the LORD,
  and on his law he meditates day and night.
He is like a tree planted by streams of water,
  which yields its fruit in season
and whose leaf does not wither.
  Whatever he does prospers.
Not so the wicked!
  They are like chaff
  that the wind blows away.
Therefore the wicked will not stand in the judgment,
  nor sinners in the assembly of the righteous.
For the LORD watches over the way of the righteous,
  but the way of the wicked will perish.

It all seems quite clear. Those who follow God and live morally excellent lives will be blessed and will prosper. Those who are wicked ... well, things don't turn out as well for them.

Here's the dilemma: When you live enough years on this earth, you discover that it is not quite that clear-cut. Sometimes scoundrels seem to be successful! Business people cook their books, lie about their competitors, over-promise and cheat their customers—and yet they continue to set profitability records year after year. Husbands cheat on their wives, and wives cheat on their husbands, and no one seems to notice. People abuse their bodies, putting the wrong stuff in them, but they come out clean as a whistle at every medical checkup. Some people seem to break every rule and get away with it.

Then there's the other side of the coin. There are fully devoted followers of Christ, real modern-day saints, champions for God, who experience painful trials and difficulties in their lives. These faithful people face financial hardship, marital breakdown, heartbreaks with their children, medical problems ... you name it. None of us has to look very far to find people who seem to be living morally excellent lives but are struggling with deep pain and sorrow.

So what's the deal? Does following God really pay? Is it worth it? Are there any real benefits associated with leading a squeaky-clean moral life?

A WIDE ANGLE VIEW

1 Tell about a time when you or someone you know tried to do the right thing for God but things seemed to go wrong. *Or*, tell about a time you watched someone (not necessary to use names) cross all kinds of moral boundaries and seemed to get away with it.

A BIBLICAL PORTRAIT

Read Psalm 73

2 In Psalm 73:1–16 the psalmist has a very specific view of life. How would you describe his outlook on *each* of the following in the psalm's first portion?

- His own life and condition

- The lives of the wicked and their condition

- God's activity in the world

3 In Psalm 73:17–28 everything changes. When the psalmist enters the sanctuary of God, the whole world looks different. How would you describe his outlook on *each* of the following in the psalm's second portion?

- His own life and condition

- The lives of the wicked and their condition

- God's activity in the world

SHARPENING THE FOCUS

Read Snapshot "The Slippery Rock Principle"

THE SLIPPERY ROCK PRINCIPLE

Have you ever tried to cross a stream by walking on moss-covered rocks just beneath the surface of the water? If you have, you know how treacherous it can be. If you haven't, you have probably watched someone try to cross a stream this way.

This is how it goes. As the person starts across, they're going slowly, choosing each stepping-stone very carefully. It is clear that their footing is precarious. They bobble a bit but regain their balance. They take another step . . . eyes riveted on the next mossy stone just under the flowing water. Partway across the stream they start to lose their balance and begin moving faster than they should. They take a big step from one submerged rock to the next and their foot slips right out from under them as it hits the slick green surface of the stone. Into the water they go with a big splash!

The moral of the story is quite simple. Those who walk on slippery rocks long enough or often enough will eventually wind up going down.

---

4 We all know people who have tried to walk on the slippery stones of moral compromise and have gotten away with it for a time. But eventually their foot slipped and they crashed. Tell about one such situation you witnessed (without using names) and reflect on the cost of their crash.

5 As sinful people, we all are tempted to live with moral compromise. In His grace, God gives us warning signs (little slips and bobbles as we try walking on mossy stones). Name some of these warning signs.

Why does God give us these warnings?

Read Snapshot "Return to the Moral High Ground"

RETURN TO THE MORAL HIGH GROUND

 We could tell stories all day long about people who walked on morally slippery ground and eventually fell. After living in raw defiance of God year after year — relationally, ethically, morally, physically, or financially — inevitably they stepped on yet another mossy stone and down they went. In that moment, families were shattered, marriages imploded, businesses went upside down, and churches were fractured. Pain beyond description was experienced, and the heart of God broke again.

God does not take delight in these moments . . . He grieves. This is why through all human history He has called out to His children playing with moral compromise, "Don't walk on slippery stones. Stay away from those moss-covered rocks. Don't get near them. Return to the moral high ground."

As followers of Jesus we need to heed these warnings. No more cutting corners. No more double-talking. No more exaggerating. No more gossip. No more "gray area" deal making. Enough with "one more quick peek" at questionable movies, magazines, and websites. Enough with padding expenses on tax forms or business expense reports. Enough with crossing sexual boundaries. Enough with arrogant attitudes. Enough with neglecting family for another business advancement. Take God's hand and walk toward moral excellence with His help and in His power. Keep your life morally clean. Don't take one more step onto one more moss-covered stone. It's time to head for the moral high ground.

6 Tell about a time in your life when you followed God's warning and left the morally slippery ground on which you were walking.

How did this change your relationship with God and others?

7 If you are willing to be vulnerable, what is an area of your life right now where you are still walking on slippery stones?

How can your group members pray for you and keep you accountable as you leave this life-pattern and seek the moral high ground?

Read Snapshot "The Final Destination Principle"

THE FINAL DESTINATION PRINCIPLE

The biggest danger is *not* that you continue with your secret, slippery-stone behavior for a few more days. It's *not* that you will be exposed and discovered. It's *not even* that you fall and face pain, scandal, embarrassment, bankruptcy, or some other consequence. Without question, the biggest danger *is* that you get away with your secret misbehavior and hidden sin. The worst possible scenario is that you fool your friends, family, spouse, small group members, church people, business associates, clients, and yourself as you carry this sin-twisted secret all the way to your grave.

If that happens, it doesn't mean that you made it. It doesn't mean you're home free. Even if you survive the slippery rocks, there's the final destination principle. The Bible says a day is coming when all human beings will stand and give an account for their moral choices before an absolutely holy God. You can dupe every person in this world and deceive yourself, but you won't fool God.

In this moment we will either pay the price of our moral debt for all we have done or we will have Jesus stand up and declare that He paid it for us. All those who have taken their whole pile of moral debt and laid it down at the foot of His blood-stained cross will be cleansed and forgiven. They will hear, "Come into My kingdom and live with Me forever." Those who have not had their moral debt paid by Jesus Christ will have to pay it on their own. This is the saddest scenario of all.

8 How does the hope of heaven and anticipation of eternal intimacy with God help us seek to live morally excellent lives?

PUTTING YOURSELF IN THE PICTURE

WATCH OUT FOR SLIPPERY STONES

We all are tempted to live with moral compromise — slippery stones are everywhere and Satan is forever seeking ways to make us trip and fall. If we are going to live morally excellent lives, we must beware of the following:

1. Areas in which we have slipped and fallen in the past.
2. Areas in which we are sure we will never fall.

Take time in the coming week to reflect in both of these directions. First, identify one or two areas where you have struggled in the past. Pray for strength to resist temptation in these areas. If you are walking on slippery stones again, call out to God and head for the moral high ground. If you need accountability, ask a strong Christian friend to help you through this process.

Second, identify one or two areas of sin that you are confident you would never struggle with. Ask God to humble your heart and allow you to keep your guard up in these areas. Often the enemy will attack in the areas of life where we are not fortified. When we say, "I would never do that," we can easily drop our guard and become a target.

MEDITATE ON HEAVEN

Read Bible passages that paint a picture of heaven and give a vision of what awaits those who have come to the Father through faith in Jesus. As you reflect on them, let the hope of the resurrection and heaven strengthen your resolve to live with moral excellence until you see Jesus face to face.

- 1 Corinthians 15:42–57
- 2 Corinthians 5:1–5
- Revelation 21:1–5

LIVING EXCELLENT RELATIONAL LIVES

REFLECTIONS FROM SESSION 2

1. What is one way you are seeking to live and walk on the moral high ground since the last time your group met?
2. There are many slippery rocks upon which we can fall. What is one area in which you feel the enemy tries to cause you to slip, and what are you doing to resist this temptation?

THE BIG PICTURE

As a young man I was greatly influenced by Dr. Gilbert Bilezikian, a New Testament scholar and one of my teachers. Over the years he became a friend, mentor, and partner in ministry. One passage of Scripture that he always taught with passionate enthusiasm was the second chapter of Acts.

This passage recounts the birth of the New Testament church and tells how the Holy Spirit moved the early followers of Jesus. The first thing that these people did was meet together, gathering in each others' homes to share their lives in deep and significant ways.

"They met together" — I like that little phrase. I've taught on it many times through my years of ministry. "They broke bread in their homes and ate together with glad and sincere hearts" (Acts 2:46). Here is my personal paraphrase of this important passage: *They took off their masks and related to each other with self-giving love.* And that was a sign that the Spirit of God was doing something real in their lives.

As I caught the biblical vision for authentic community, I ached to be a part of a church like that, so different from what I had known in the church where I grew up. Don't get me wrong. The people in my childhood church were kind and they had faith, but there was no sense of community, vulnerability, or authenticity. They filed in, attended services, and headed out without their lives really intersecting with each other.

When the Acts 2 vision of relational connections started to sink into my mind and my soul, it captured me. My heart longed to be part of a community where we could take off the masks and really give ourselves in love and support to each other. It was this vision that caused me to change my career plans and devote the rest of my life to building an authentic biblically functioning community. To be honest, decades later, it is still one of the driving passions of my life.

The Bible gives us some beautiful glimpses of the first-century church. It is clear that believers gathered in large groups and also in small clusters. They met in public settings and also in the intimacy of homes. They needed both kinds of experiences and so do we.

In this session our focus is on living excellent relational lives. Of course, there are many ways to do this. In this study we will be looking at how we grow in our relational lives as we gather in small clusters with other believers. Those believers who commit to consistent connection with a small group of Christ followers will quickly discover that their capacity for relational excellence accelerates. The truth is, there are some kinds of growth and maturity that happen best in a small group experience.

A WIDE ANGLE VIEW

1   Most of us have seen examples of people who go to church, follow the routine, and go home with no real connection with other believers. As a matter of fact, many of us have had seasons in our lives when we have functioned this way. What do we miss out on when we settle for this kind of church experience?

In the same way, most of us have had times when we have deeply engaged with other believers and taken the risk of being in an authentic Christian community. What do we gain when we seek this kind of connection with other followers of Jesus?

A BIBLICAL PORTRAIT

Read Acts 2:42–47; 1 John 4:11–12; and James 5:13–16

2 What were some of the *practices* that marked the life of the first-century church, and how do you see these alive or missing in the church today?

3 What were some of the *attitudes* that marked the life of the first-century church, and how do you see these alive or missing in the church today?

SHARPENING THE FOCUS

Read Snapshot "Love and Affirmation"

LOVE AND AFFIRMATION

Testimony: *"I enjoy gathering for worship services with a large group. I feel inspired. I learn. But I don't feel a depth of love from a big congregation. When I'm going through a tough time I can go to church services for a month and nobody says 'I love you.'"*

This testimony is not an incrimination of the church. It is simply a reflection of how large-group dynamics work. It does not matter if your local church meets with 125 people or 7,000 people weekly, worship services don't necessarily create a place for love and affirmation on a personal level.

This is one of the reasons God calls us to deepen our relational lives in small groups. When we gather consistently in more intimate clusters, we can express love and affirmation to each other. There is time to listen, extend a touch, speak words of blessing, and tell each other, "You matter to God and you matter to me!"

---

4 How have you found a small group setting to be a natural place to express and receive love and affirmation?

What can you do as a small group to create more space for expressing love and affirmation to each other?

Read Snapshot "Life Application"

LIFE APPLICATION

Testimony: *"I get a lot out of church services. I almost always leave with some truth or challenge that impacts my life. But when I get in my small group and we talk about what we learned in the church services, when I hear what others learned and how they are applying it, the Spirit uses these interactions to take me to a deeper place of growth and application."*

There is just something about hearing what God has said to others, and discovering how they are applying what they have learned, that clarifies and refines what God is saying to us. This is the wonder of community. When we live and think in isolation, we miss out on the rich insights of other believers. When we gather with a small group of Christ-followers, speak with open hearts, and listen with open ears, our faith deepens.

5 A small group is a wonderful setting to speak openly and honestly about what we are learning from sermons and our own study of Scripture. How can the thoughts and insights of others help to shape and deepen personal life application?

Read Snapshot "Accountability"

ACCOUNTABILITY

Testimony: *"I can slip in and out of church services for months and avoid people. I can go on with my life relatively unchanged. But in my small group, people get in my face ... in a loving way! They ask me, 'Are you spending time with Jesus?' 'Are you reading your Bible?' 'Are you making good business decisions?' In my small group I can't get away with much, and I love it."*

No Christ-follower can grow to full maturity without accountability. And there will be no accountability unless we seek it out. When we seek it out, we must hold ourselves to the rigors of it. One of the best places this can happen is in a small group of believers whom we trust, who know us, and who love us.

6 How has participation in a small group raised the bar for accountability in your life?

What steps can you take as a group to increase the level of accountability both when you are together and between gatherings?

Read Snapshot "Major Life Decisions"

MAJOR LIFE DECISIONS

Testimony: *"For years I attended church and grew in my faith. But there were times when I would sit in worship services during a major crossroads moment of life and wish one of these wise people would come to my side and help me sort things out. I'm sure if I would have grabbed someone and asked them to help me, they would have said yes, but I never dared. When I finally got into a small group, I had an instant team of Christ-followers who gladly shared their insights and prayed for me when I was making big life decisions. I wish I had joined a small group years ago."*

On a handful of occasions during my years of preaching, I have asked the congregation, "Stand if you're at a major crossroads in your life — vocationally, relationally, financially, whatever." Typically about a third of the congregation stands. I am always amazed. In those moments I find myself hoping and praying that these people are in a small group, making space to help each other find wisdom and direction at these critical times.

7 If you are facing a major decision or crossroads moment of life, what is it and how can your group members pray, support, and bring wisdom?

Read Snapshot "Confession"

CONFESSION

Testimony: *"I meet with a group of men every Friday morning for breakfast. We've grown to love and trust each other so much so that we are completely open about our shortcomings and mess-ups. No masks! I actually never thought something like this was possible. We actually confess our sins to each other, we keep each other accountable, we challenge each other, and we help each other to stay on God's path."*

In a small group we can take off our masks. We can encourage, challenge, and love each other on a level that just can't happen in a gathered worship setting. In the book of James we read these challenging countercultural words: "Therefore confess your sins to each other and pray for each other so that you may be healed" (James 5:16). One of the best places to do this is in a small group.

8 What are the potential risks and dangers of confessing your sins and struggles in a small group setting?

What are the values and benefits of becoming a group that can humbly confess areas of struggle, sin, and brokenness?

PUTTING YOURSELF IN THE PICTURE

PRAYING THE SCRIPTURE

Since Acts 2:42–47 is such a formative passage of the Bible, take time to pray through it in the coming week. Read the passage slowly and identify what the early believers did and the characteristics that marked their community. Then pray for each of these practices and attitudes to become part of your life. Use the space below to direct your study and prayer (two examples have already been provided):

Verse	Lesson	Prayer
42	Devoted to teaching	Lord, help me be a student of Your Word
42	Devoted to fellowship	Teach me to engage in fellowship

AFFIRMATION

As you engage in community with a small group, you get to know a lot about the group members. With time you know frailties, struggles, and sins. You also know strengths, areas of victory, and gifting. Spend time this week writing a note, sending an email, or texting a group member. Write with one intention in mind: affirmation. Identify where you see God at work in their life—and give a word of blessing.

LIVING
EXCELLENT
FINANCIAL
LIVES

REFLECTIONS FROM SESSION 3

1. Since the last time your group gathered, how have you been trying to incorporate some of the practices or attitudes of the early church (Acts 2:42 – 47) into your life and relational connections?

2. As you have reflected on the values of being part of a small group community (Love and Affirmation, Life Application, Accountability, Wisdom in Making Life Decisions, and Confession), how can your group go deeper in one of these areas?

THE BIG PICTURE

Many years ago we built a home just a few blocks from the Willow Creek Community Church campus. After much planning, time, energy, and anticipation, we were just a few days from actually moving in; in fact, we had already taken many of our things to the new place. It was exciting!

Then two nights before the move-in, something unsettling happened. Thieves broke in, ransacked our home, and stole things that belonged and mattered to us. As we walked around the house processing what had happened, all sorts of feelings swept through our hearts.

I remember feeling violated. It is hard to put into words, but there was a sense of intrusion into our lives. Someone had taken what was ours. I found myself thinking, "Who did this?

Who is so brazenly self-centered and uncaring that they would invade our lives in this way?"

If you have ever had someone steal from you, break into your home, or take what belongs to you, you know the vast array of feelings that come with such an experience.

A WIDE ANGLE VIEW

1 If you have been robbed or had something stolen from you, how were you impacted? How did it make you feel?

A BIBLICAL PORTRAIT

Read Malachi 3:6–12 and Proverbs 3:9–10

2 How does God feel about the behavior of His people in light of what you read in Malachi 3:6–12?

3 What is God calling His people to do in these passages?

What does God say will happen if His people follow His call to live with generosity?

SHARPENING THE FOCUS

Read Snapshot "The Heart Check"

THE HEART CHECK

God calls His people to give the first 10 percent (tithe) of all they earn back to Him. It is as simple as that. The tithe belongs to God. But it does not end there. After we have given these "first fruits," we are called to live with open hearts and hands. That means we should also make the other 90 percent available for God's use, as He would prompt us.

All through the Old and New Testaments this message is reinforced. Jesus said, "For where your treasure is, there your heart will be also" (Matt. 6:21). Tithing isn't fundamentally about money. It's about the condition of your heart before God. When God is your greatest treasure, giving the tithe, and offerings beyond that, comes naturally.

When we see the tithing principle against the backdrop of a blood-stained cross, we realize that we ought to honor Christ no matter how much it costs us. God gave His best. Jesus left glory and died on a Roman cross. He has given us new life through faith in Him. We ought to gladly offer this minimum requirement of 10 percent with joy. When our heart is right, generous giving follows.

4 Why do you think God calls us to give our first 10 percent back to Him?

How does a person's pattern of giving reflect the condition of his or her heart?

5 What specific growth steps will help us expand our hearts so that giving a tithe and offerings (gifts above the first 10 percent) is a natural response of love?

Read Snapshot "The Gut Check"

THE GUT CHECK

A gut check is about having the courage to examine our character to ensure we are taking the practical steps needed to honor God with our finances. If we are going to get on board with living lives of financial excellence, it will mean rearranging our personal money management disciplines.

In other words, we will have to sit down with our financial records and a calculator and figure out how much we actually earn through various revenue streams. Then, based on our total income and investments, we can determine how much represents a full tithe. This takes guts. It takes character. It takes good old-fashioned discipline and attention to detail. It takes follow-through. A heart check without a gut check is a setup for hypocrisy.

6 If a person has a heart for God and wants to give Him the tithe, and even offerings, but never does a serious gut check, what might happen?

How might a serious personal evaluation of our financial lives bring our hearts and actions into sync and deepen our faith?

7 Take five minutes on your own for the three bulleted exercises, and then as a group discuss the follow-up questions:

- **Do an initial gut check.** Think through your income over the past two or three months. Then think about what you have given to God's work in this same time period. Be as honest with yourself as you can. Are you tithing? Are you giving offerings?
- **Reflect on your heart** over the past two or three months. Have you been giving joyfully and generously? Have you been reflecting on how much God has done (and is doing) for you? How is your giving a reflection of your heart?
- **Spend a moment in silent prayer.** If you have been living in joyful obedience to God in

your financial life, praise Him and ask for strength to continue. If this area is a struggle presently, pray for your heart to love God more deeply and for your life to reflect this love in the way you give.

What happened in your heart during this gut check time?

What is God saying to you about how you view Him and how this impacts the way you handle finances?

Read Snapshot "The Faith Check"

THE FAITH CHECK

Once we do a heart check and a gut check, it is time for a faith check. The only way we will consistently use money to honor God is when we are walking and living by faith.

When we live by faith we are confident that God can provide for all of our needs, even when times are tough. When faith rules our hearts we know that God can "throw open the floodgates of heaven" and "prevent pests from devouring our crops." In other words, instead of being anxious about the stock market or the latest economic report, we can live each day with confidence, knowing that God is on the throne and will watch over His children.

8 What are some financial situations that can shake our faith and cause us to become fearful rather than faithful?

9 What helps you maintain a faithful heart and generous hands even in hard times?

PUTTING YOURSELF IN THE PICTURE

Gut Check

Sometime in the coming week, set aside an hour or two to walk through the process laid out in question 7 (pages 38–39). If you are married, do this as a couple. Really look at your resources and your giving patterns, and seek God's leading as you do.

Heart Check

A big part of a heart check is making sure we remember all God has done for us. As we reflect on His abundant goodness and amazing grace, giving back makes sense. Spend time making a list of the many blessings God has given you. As you do this, ask the Holy Spirit to grow your desire to give back joyfully and gladly.

Spiritual Blessings . . .

The Gift of People . . .

Material Things I Enjoy . . .

LIVING
EXCELLENT
DIRECTIONAL
LIVES

REFLECTIONS FROM SESSION 4

1. If you did a financial gut check since the last time your group met, what did you learn about yourself and your commitment to be a joyful and generous giver?
2. How is your heart growing more in love with God, and how is this impacting the way you understand personal finances?

THE BIG PICTURE

When facing a big decision, the best place to get input is from God Himself. Our all-wise God loves to give His leading freely and generously ... if only we would ask.

At the critical crossroads of our lives, it is time to get on our knees, look up to heaven, lift our hands, and say, "God, I need your direction. I don't want to move forward without Your wisdom and guidance. I am not willing to rely on my own insight or the input of a few friends. I must have You in the equation."

Sadly, when many people approach key intersections of their lives they try to figure things out on their own. They have no framework for obtaining quality, reliable, and desperately needed input. Instead of looking to God, they rely on a combination of human intuition, a little life experience, input from talk show hosts, New Age authors, and friends who mean well but don't know very much. The end result is often tragic.

God wants us to know that we can do better than that. He has all kinds of wisdom and insight that He is waiting to share with us—we just need to avail ourselves of it. Nothing would please Him more than to steer His children in the most constructive direction we can go. He takes delight in coming alongside of us at every critical intersection of life to help us make the right call.

A WIDE ANGLE VIEW

1 Tell about a time you had to make a decision and failed to ask God for wisdom and direction. How did things turn out?

Tell about a time you really slowed down and looked to God for His direction. What means did God use to guide you?

A BIBLICAL PORTRAIT

Read James 1:5–8; Psalm 119:105; Romans 8:14; Proverbs 11:14; and Colossians 4:3

2 According to these passages, what are some of the ways that God gives direction to His children?

How have you experienced one of these direction-giving encounters with God?

SHARPENING THE FOCUS

Read Snapshot "Faith Instead of Doubt"

FAITH INSTEAD OF DOUBT

If we're considering asking God for guidance at a critical intersection, we have to demonstrate faith in Him. This means humbling ourselves and crying out, "God, I have concluded Your wisdom is higher than my own. Your guidance is trustworthier than any I'm going to be able to patch together from worldly sources. I'm looking to You and to You alone. So, when Your direction comes, I will follow it as best I can. I will apply it to my life, believing that You will lead me in the way I should go." That's faith!

The apostle James says we need to ask for God's direction with faith-filled hearts and without doubting. In other words, we are to trust God with single-mindedness, not double-mindedness. God takes delight every time one of His children asks for His leading and confidently believes He will give it. Our faith releases His wisdom to flow freely into our lives.

James speaks with piercing clarity, "If any of you lacks wisdom, he should ask God, who gives generously to all without finding fault, and it will be given to him. But when he asks, he must believe and not doubt, because he who doubts is like a wave of the sea, blown and tossed by the wind" (James 1:5–6). In modern language we might say, "Don't try to approach God for guidance when you are not serious about it. Don't come to a major decision and try to cover all the bases by tuning into *Oprah*, reading a fortune cookie, flipping a coin, rubbing a rabbit's foot, talking to the guys at the club over a beer, and, oh, yeah, throwing up a prayer to God."

That is being double-minded, and James says that directional excellence is not attained that way. Instead, we come to God and ask for wisdom, believing He has exactly what we need. And, when He gives us direction, we should follow it with confidence.

3

Why do you think God is so concerned that we live with confident, rock-solid faith in Him and not place part of our faith in the "wisdom" of the world?

Through your years as a follower of Jesus, what has strengthened and fortified your faith in His ability to guide you?

Read Snapshot "Biblical Direction"

BIBLICAL DIRECTION

God's primary guidance in our daily lives comes through His Word, the Bible. Psalm 119:105 teaches us that His Word is a lamp and a light that shows us our next step. Indeed, we would all stumble around in the dark or wind up in a ditch if it weren't for the light of truth recorded there.

For instance, if we want to know the ground rules of morality, we need only read the Ten Commandments (Ex. 20) to know that we should honor our fathers and mothers, that we should not kill, steal, lie, commit adultery, or covet. The Bible says these are the building blocks of society. This is how to build a family. This is how to build individual relationships with integrity. God is not playing hide-and-seek with us. His teaching is straightforward and clear.

It's often said that 90 percent of all we need to know has already been written in the Bible. If we read it every day and saturate our minds with God's truth, letting it wash over us, we will have the directional wisdom we need when we come to life's critical crossroads.

Describe a time when the simple, clear teaching of the Bible gave you the direction you needed to press forward and follow God's will for your life.

5 How can daily study of God's written Word prepare you for most situations you will face in life?

What are some practical ways we can develop a pattern of daily Bible study to help us gain heavenly wisdom and direction in our lives?

Read Snapshot "Holy Spirit Promptings"

HOLY SPIRIT PROMPTINGS

Another remarkable way God guides His people is through promptings of His Holy Spirit. Sometimes when we arrive at a critical crossroads we need specific direction beyond the general teaching of the Bible. These promptings of the Spirit always agree with the teaching of Scripture, but with added personalized guidance.

Those who fly private airplanes know that there are established airways that almost everybody flies . . . they are like interstates in the sky. But sometimes pilots get confused and wonder if they are headed in the right direction. When this happens, they can call air traffic control and request what are known as *vectors*. Within seconds, a voice will come over the headphones and give specific direction. Sometimes the controller will say, "You are right on course." Other times the controller will say, "You're twenty degrees to the left of target. Bring it around to the right and you will be back on track."

Promptings from the Holy Spirit are a lot like receiving vectors from an air traffic controller. We don't hear an audible voice like pilots hear over their headphones, but if we learn to develop a heightened sensitivity to the Spirit's promptings, we can become very adept at knowing when He is saying, "You are right on course," or, "Move a few degrees in another direction." What a comfort to know that God speaks and directs in this way.

6

Tell about a time you felt God's prompting and heard the gentle voice of the Holy Spirit directing you. Be sure to tell how you responded to the Spirit's leading and how this impacted your life direction.

Read Snapshot "Other People"

OTHER PEOPLE

Another way God leads us is through the counsel of wise people. Proverbs 11:14 says, "Many advisors make victory sure." When we are facing a critical decision, it is wise to identify a spiritually mature Christ follower who has faced a similar situation and navigated it wisely.

We can ask strategic questions like: How did you handle this life situation? What were the dangers you thought about? How did God guide you through this time in your life? What input would you give me? After asking these questions, you might even want to invite them to take a moment, right then and there, to pray for you.

7 Who has God placed in your life with a deep faith and real wisdom, and how might they act as a sounding board for directional excellence?

8 How might your small group become a community of wisdom-givers that God could use to guide you?

If you have an area in which you need wisdom and direction today, invite your group members to communicate their wisdom and sense of God's direction for you.

Read Snapshot "Circumstances"

CIRCUMSTANCES

From time to time God will clearly open or close a door to help us follow Him. This kind of leading needs to be approached with care and wisdom. Some people give far too much credence to circumstances and far too little to the Bible, Holy Spirit promptings, and the wisdom of godly people. Those who base too much of their life-direction on circumstances tend to go wherever the wind blows ... and this is not healthy. But there are times, as we use the other spiritual tools for directional excellence, when God might close a door or open another one (Col. 4:3; 1 Cor. 16:9; 2 Cor. 2:12). We can see His leading in these moments.

---

9 Tell about a time God clearly closed a door and gave you life direction through it.

Tell about a time you sensed God had opened a door for you and you walked through it.

PUTTING YOURSELF IN THE PICTURE

TEN CLEAR DIRECTIVES

The Bible contains many teachings that give us clear and healthy direction for our lives. One of the greatest of these passages is Exodus 20 — the Ten Commandments.

Take time this week to read Exodus 20:1 – 17. Reflect on each of these clear teachings of Scripture and ask the Holy Spirit to stir your heart and prompt you if in any way you are living out of sync with them.

If you want to go a bit deeper into the spirit of the Ten Commandments, read Jesus' teachings in Matthew 5:17 – 30.

GET QUIET

The Holy Spirit often whispers. (If you don't believe this, read 1 Kings 19:11 – 13.) So, block out 15 – 30 minutes in the coming week and commit to unplug. Turn off the TV, the radio, your phone, your iPod, and all other potential noisemakers. Go somewhere you won't be interrupted. Be quiet before God, asking the Holy Spirit to nudge, prompt, and give any direction the Father wants you to receive. It might be helpful to have a note card and pen or pencil handy. Wait on God and listen. If you feel a nudge and it is consistent with the general teaching of the Bible, follow it, and see where God takes you.

LIVING
EXCELLENT
ETERNAL
LIVES

REFLECTIONS FROM SESSION 5

1. If you have been studying the Bible and seeking God's leading over the past week, what is one truth from the Scriptures that has helped you discover God's direction for your life?
2. Since the last time your group met, tell about a prompting from the Holy Spirit, an influential encounter with someone, or some circumstance you believe God is using to give direction in your life at this time.

THE BIG PICTURE

Anyone who lived in the Middle East during the Old Testament or New Testament eras understood that the metaphor of wildflowers was commonly used to paint a picture of the brevity and frailty of life. This theme comes up numerous times in the Bible:

Man born of woman
*   is of few days and full of trouble.*
He springs up like a flower and withers away;
*   like a fleeting shadow, he does not endure. (Job 14:1–2)*

As for man, his days are like grass,
*   he flourishes like a flower of the field;*
the wind blows over it and it is gone,
*   and its place remembers it no more. (Ps. 103:15–16)*

But the one who is rich should take pride in his low position, because he will pass away like a wild flower. For the sun rises with scorching heat and withers the plant; its blossom falls and its beauty is destroyed. In the same way, the rich man will fade away even while he goes about his business. (James 1:10–11)

Spring rains would fall and almost overnight the rocky hillsides in Palestine would look like an artist's palette. Rich, deep colors would spill all over the hillsides as wildflowers blossomed. It was a sight to behold. Then, the desert winds would blow with furnace-like heat. The wildflowers would shrivel up and the Monet-like landscapes would transform into a dull tangle of brown leaves and twisted stems.

These flowers become a picture of life. One day a woman is busily going about her activities and the next day people are streaming by her casket saying, "I just talked to her the other day." One day a man is committing to a ten-year strategic plan at work. The next day his family and friends are putting together plans for his funeral.

Death often comes suddenly and unexpectedly. There is a frailty to this existence. We can be like wildflowers that spring up and adorn the desert, but before you know it, this life is over.

A WIDE ANGLE VIEW

1 Tell about a time you were struck by the frailty and brevity of life. How did this moment of insight impact the way you view eternity?

A BIBLICAL PORTRAIT

Read Ephesians 2:8–9 and Titus 3:4–7

2 In this life, almost everything has to be earned. Even many Christians live with a sense that they have to

work for God's favor and love. How do these passages correct the errant human tendency to believe we have to earn our forgiveness?

Read John 14:6; Acts 4:11–12; Romans 10:9–10; and John 1:12–13

3

How does a sinful person find cleansing from sin and gain the assurance that heaven will be their home?

SHARPENING THE FOCUS

Read Snapshot "A Glorious and Undeserved Gift"

A GLORIOUS AND UNDESERVED GIFT

Throughout the entire Bible we learn that the grace of God is extended as a glorious and undeserved gift, offered freely to all who will believe in Jesus and receive His grace. The hope of heaven is not reserved for some special class of people who are inordinately pious. People of the most humble of circumstances can put their hand in the hand of Jesus Christ, have their sins forgiven, and join His honored family.

For it is by grace you have been saved, through faith—and this not from yourselves, it is the gift of God—not by works, so that no one can boast. (Eph. 2:8–9)

But when the kindness and love of God our Savior appeared, he saved us, not because of righteous things we had done, but because of his mercy. He saved us through the washing of rebirth and renewal by the Holy Spirit, whom he poured out on us generously through Jesus Christ our Savior, so that, having been justified by his grace, we might become heirs having the hope of eternal life. (Titus 3:4–7)

Forgiveness, cleansing, a restored relationship with God, and heaven all have one thing in common . . . they are undeserved. It is only by God's grace, only through His initiation, and only because of His seeking love that we can live with hope for today and eternity.

---

4 Describe the first time it sank deep into your soul that salvation is not based on your good works or personal merits, but on the amazing grace of a loving God.

5 Forgiveness and heaven are underserved gifts given from the hands of a loving God. How does this truth impact:

- How you worship God?

- How you share the love of God with others?

- How you respond when you stumble and fall into sin?

- How you view people who are living neck-deep in sin and rebellion?

- Other aspects of your life and faith?

What is one practical step you can take in response to your awareness of this truth?

Read Snapshot "The Way to Heaven"

THE WAY TO HEAVEN

Heaven is a glorious and undeserved gift. But it is not guaranteed to all people. We must *receive* the gift . . . it is not forced on us. We do not earn salvation and heaven, but we receive them when we embrace Jesus Christ. This is expressed many ways in the New Testament:

> *"Yet to all who received him, to those who believed in his name, he gave the right to become children of God—children born not of natural descent, nor of human decision or a husband's will, but born of God." (John 1:12–13)*

If we confess our sins, he is faithful and just and will forgive us our sins and purify us from all unrighteousness. (1 John 1:9)

That if you confess with your mouth, "Jesus is Lord," and believe in your heart that God raised him from the dead, you will be saved. For it is with your heart that you believe and are justified, and it is with your mouth that you confess and are saved. (Rom. 10:9–10)

The Bible does not teach a universal salvation for all people. What God's Word says is that all those who receive Jesus become children of God. Those who confess their sins and accept God's grace offered in Christ are purified. Those who believe in the Savior will be saved. The gift is extended to all people; those who receive it become children of God and their eternity is secure.

---

6 Tell about when you first believed in Jesus, accepted His forgiveness, and became part of God's family.

7 The message of God's love and grace is truly amazing. The hope of heaven is glorious. What are some of the ways we can communicate this good news to friends and family members who have not yet embraced Jesus?

8 Who is one person you are praying will come to faith in Jesus, and how are you trying to reach out with the love and message of Jesus?

How can your group members support you, pray for you, and encourage you in your efforts to share God's message of grace with this person?

Read Snapshot "The Glory of Heaven"

THE GLORY OF HEAVEN

The Bible uses all kinds of images to help us glimpse the glory that awaits us in heaven. But this side of eternity, we can't begin to imagine how amazing it will be. Words and pictures can't convey the full wonder of heaven, but they give us a taste of what lies ahead. The apostle Paul tells us that in heaven we will be imperishable, sin will be gone, death will be dead, and we will experience the victory of Jesus (1 Cor. 15:50–57).

In John's revelation we get another view of heaven. We will be with Jesus forever, all hunger and thirst will be gone, we will be protected, and every tear will be wiped away (Rev. 7:15–17). Later we learn that in heaven God will be with us, the glory of the Lord will be our source of light, all impurity will be purged away, and we will be invited to serve the Savior who gave His life for us (Rev. 21:22–22:5). There are even pictures of precious stones, golden streets, and beauty beyond human comprehension (Rev. 21:18–21). These human descriptions are meant to capture our imagination and inspire our heart. Heaven will be better than our wildest dreams!

Read 1 Corinthians 15:50–57; Revelation 7:15–17; and Revelation 21:18–22:5

 When you think about heaven, what excites you most about going there when this life ends?

How does the hope of heaven inspire you to live for Jesus today?

PUTTING YOURSELF IN THE PICTURE

THANK-YOU CARD

Most of us learned as children that when someone gave us a gift it was proper to write a thank-you note. Take time in the coming week to write a note or letter to God. Thank Him for the best gift you have ever received. Let Him know that you appreciate His grace, you are thankful for His sacrifice, and you are excited about the hope of heaven.

SHARING THE WAY

Once we have found the way to heaven, it makes sense to let others know that God's grace is available to them as well. Pray for boldness and opportunity to tell someone about your journey to Jesus. Let them know how you embraced and accepted Him. Share how Jesus has transformed, and continues to transform, your life. Then tell them how they can begin a new life through faith in Jesus Christ.

LEADER'S NOTES

Leading a Bible discussion—especially for the first time—can make you feel both nervous and excited. If you are nervous, realize that you are in good company. Many biblical leaders, such as Moses, Joshua, and the apostle Paul, felt nervous and inadequate to lead others (see, for example, 1 Cor. 2:3). Yet God's grace was sufficient for them, just as it will be for you.

Some excitement is also natural. Your leadership is a gift to the others in the group. Keep in mind, however, that other group members also share responsibility for the group. Your role is simply to stimulate discussion by asking questions and encouraging people to respond. The suggestions listed below can help you to be an effective leader.

PREPARING TO LEAD

1. Ask God to help you understand and apply the passage to your own life. Unless that happens, you will not be prepared to lead others.
2. Carefully work through each question in the study guide. Meditate and reflect on the passage as you formulate your answers.
3. Familiarize yourself with the Leader's Notes for each session. These will help you understand the purpose of the session and will provide valuable information about the questions in the session. The Leader's Notes are not intended to be read to the group. These notes are primarily for your use as a group leader and for your preparation. However, when you find a section that relates well to your group, you may want to read a brief portion or encourage them to read this section at another time.
4. Pray for the various members of the group. Ask God to use these sessions to make you better disciples of Jesus Christ.
5. Before the first session, make sure each person has a study guide. Encourage them to prepare beforehand for each session.

LEADING THE SESSION

1. Begin the session on time. If people realize that the session begins on schedule, they will work harder to arrive on time.

2. At the beginning of your first time together, explain that these sessions are designed to be discussions, not lectures. Encourage everyone to participate, but realize some may be hesitant to speak during the first few sessions.

3. Don't be afraid of silence. People in the group may need time to think before responding.

4. Avoid answering your own questions. If necessary, rephrase a question until it is clearly understood. Even an eager group will quickly become passive and silent if they think the leader will do most of the talking.

5. Encourage more than one answer to each question. Ask, "What do the rest of you think?" or "Anyone else?" until several people have had a chance to respond.

6. Try to be affirming whenever possible. Let people know you appreciate their insights into the passage.

7. Never reject an answer. If it is clearly wrong, ask, "Which verse led you to that conclusion?" Or let the group handle the problem by asking them what they think about the question.

8. Avoid going off on tangents. If people wander off course, gently bring them back to the passage being considered.

9. Conclude your time together with conversational prayer. Ask God to help you apply those things that you learned in the session.

10. End on time. This will be easier if you control the pace of the discussion by not spending too much time on some questions or too little on others.

We encourage all small group leaders to use *Leading Life-Changing Small Groups* (Zondervan) by Bill Donahue and the Willow Creek Small Group Team while leading their group. Developed and used by Willow Creek Community Church, this guide is an excellent resource for training and equipping followers of Christ to effectively lead small groups. It includes valuable information on how to utilize fun and creative relationship-building exercises for your group; how to plan your meeting; how to share the leadership load by identifying, developing, and working with an "apprentice leader"; and how to find creative ways to do group prayer. In addition, the book includes material and tips on handling potential conflicts and difficult personalities, forming group covenants, inviting new members, improving listening skills, studying the Bible, and much more. Using *Leading Life-Changing Small Groups* will help you create a group that members love to be a part of.

Now let's discuss the different elements of this small group study guide and how to use them for the session portion of your group meeting.

THE BIG PICTURE

Each session will begin with a short story or overview of the lesson theme. This is called "The Big Picture" because it introduces the central theme of the session. You will need to read this section as a group or have group members read it on their own before discussion begins. Here are three ways you can approach this section of the small group session:

- As the group leader, read this section out loud for the whole group and then move into the questions in the next section, "A Wide Angle View." (You might read the first week, but then use the other two options below to encourage group involvement.)
- Ask a group member to volunteer to read this section for the group. This allows another group member to participate. It is best to ask someone in advance to give them time to read over the section before reading it to the group. It is also good to ask someone to volunteer, and not to assign this task. Some people do not feel comfortable reading in front of a group. After a group member has read this section out loud, move into the discussion questions.
- Allow time at the beginning of the session for each person to read this section silently. If you do this, be sure to allow enough time for everyone to finish reading so they can think about what they've read and be ready for meaningful discussion.

A WIDE ANGLE VIEW

This section includes one or more questions that move the group into a general discussion of the session topic. These questions are designed to help group members begin discussing the topic in an open and honest manner. Once the topic of the lesson has been established, move on to the Bible passage for the session.

A BIBLICAL PORTRAIT

This portion of the session includes a Scripture reading and one or more questions that help group members see how the theme of the session is rooted and based in biblical teaching. The Scripture reading can be handled just like "The Big Picture" section:

You can read it for the group, have a group member read it, or allow time for silent reading. Make sure everyone has a Bible or that you have Bibles available for those who need them. Once you have read the passage, ask the question(s) in this section so that group members can dig into the truth of the Bible.

SHARPENING THE FOCUS

The majority of the discussion questions for the session are in this section. These questions are practical and help group members apply biblical teaching to their daily lives.

SNAPSHOTS

The "Snapshots" in each session help prepare group members for discussion. These anecdotes give additional insight to the topic being discussed. Each "Snapshot" should be read at a designated point in the session. This is clearly marked in the session as well as in the Leader's Notes. Again, follow the same format as you do with "The Big Picture" section and the "Biblical Portrait" section: Either you read the anecdote, have a group member volunteer to read, or provide time for silent reading. However you approach this section, you will find these anecdotes very helpful in triggering lively dialogue and moving discussion in a meaningful direction.

PUTTING YOURSELF IN THE PICTURE

Here's where you roll up your sleeves and put the truth into action. This portion is very practical and action-oriented. At the end of each session there will be suggestions for one or two ways group members can put what they've just learned into practice. Review the action goals at the end of each session and challenge group members to work on one or more of them in the coming week.

You will find follow-up questions for the "Putting Yourself in the Picture" section at the beginning of the next week's session. Starting with the second week, there will be time set aside at the beginning of the session to look back and talk about how you have tried to apply God's Word in your life since your last time together.

PRAYER

You will want to open and close your small group with a time of prayer. Occasionally, there will be specific direction within a session for how you can do this. Most of the time, however, you will need to decide the best place to stop and pray. You may want to pray or have a group member volunteer to begin the lesson with a prayer. Or you might want to read "The Big Picture" and discuss the "Wide Angle View" questions before opening in prayer. In some cases, it might be best to open in prayer after you have read the Bible passage. You need to decide where you feel an opening prayer best fits for your group.

When opening in prayer, think in terms of the session theme and pray for group members (including yourself) to be responsive to the truth of Scripture and the working of the Holy Spirit. If you have seekers in your group (people investigating Christianity but not yet believers), be sensitive to your expectations for group prayer. Seekers may not yet be ready to take part in group prayer.

Be sure to close your group with a time of prayer as well. One option is for you to pray for the entire group. Or you might allow time for group members to offer audible prayers that others can agree with in their hearts. Another approach would be to allow a time of silence for one-on-one prayers with God and then to close this time with a simple "Amen."

LIVING EXCELLENT SPIRITUAL LIVES

MALACHI 1:6—14

INTRODUCTION

In Malachi 1 the prophet asks the people of his day, "How should a human being respond to the excellent nature and activities of God?" What kind of response, what kind of worship offering, and what kind of lamb do you bring to an excellent God? In a sense, he is asking, "What does an excellent spiritual life look like?"

Malachi would say, "Hint—a blemished lamb is not the right answer. The one leaning against the fence ready to die—don't bring that one. The blind one, the crippled one, the one not worth anything at the market—don't bring the wrong kind of lamb to the One who gave His best for you. Don't do it."

God deserves our absolute best. We are to bring Him our best commitment, our best affection, and our best service. We are to use our gifts and abilities for His glory. Anything short of this reveals that we have not yet realized the glory and honor of this God we worship.

THE BIG PICTURE

Take time to read this introduction with the group. There are suggestions for how this can be done in the beginning of the leader's section.

A WIDE ANGLE VIEW

Question One The more things change, the more they stay the same! We are no different than the people in Malachi's day. They brought sick lambs but we are tempted to doze through a worship service. They cut corners with their offerings and so can we. Take time to honestly look at some of the ways that followers of Christ can still be tempted to bring their second best (or worst) to God.

A Biblical Portrait

Read Malachi 1:6–14

Question Two Malachi calls us to excellent spiritual lives in response to the God who deserves our praise. Why? Because:

- He is the Lord Almighty. (vv. 6, 8, 9, 10, 13)
- His name is great among the nations ... from the rising to the setting of the sun. (v. 11)
- In every place He is worshiped. (v. 11)
- He is a great king. (v. 14)
- His name is feared among the nations. (v. 14)

Question Three Get the picture: These people pick out a lamb, run quickly to the temple, put it on the altar, and say to God, "Here's your worship offering. Hope you like it." The lamb is sick, has puss in its eyes, and is about to drop over dead. Malachi says, "Just try passing that off as a good gift to a political leader ... they would see right through your offering."

Malachi was sent by God to tell the people that God doesn't like such behavior. He doesn't like it at all. In fact, the whole deal offends Him to the point where Malachi says, "Better you bring no lamb at all than you bring a blemished one. Shut the temple doors before you ever try that stunt again."

This is not to say that God expects perfection from us. He knows our frailties and weaknesses. It is simply a call to seek excellence in every part of our lives, including our spiritual lives.

Sharpening the Focus

Read Snapshot "Your Best Commitment" before Question 4

Question Four The God of heaven has poured out His love on each of us who are followers of Jesus. The gift of His only Son is the apex of this revelation of love, but there is so much more. In the book of Ephesians we are told that God "has blessed us in the heavenly realms with every spiritual blessing in Christ" (1:3). As a group, list and celebrate the amazing storehouse of blessings God has given us, including the fruit of the Spirit, the body of Christ (fellowship), spiritual gifts, and so much more.

Read Snapshot "Your Best Affection" before Question 6

Question Six Expressions of spiritual affection may vary. Perhaps it's writing letters or poetry to God, reading psalms to

Him, or singing worship songs. But when we truly understand the quality of God's love, we want to return excellent love back to Him. We want to give the best "lamb" we have.

When this all started making sense to me, I responded to an excellent God by wanting to make an excellent commitment, a more sincere expression of affection. I started getting very creative. I hope you do too.

Read Snapshot "The Best Contributions of Your Skills and Talents" before Question 8

Question Eight We all have more to offer than we realize. The excellent God we worship has placed gifts and abilities in each of us. Some of your group members might be shy and reserved about actually saying, "I have a gift," or, "I have something to offer." If they are, you might want to point out their abilities and gifts and help them celebrate them . . . maybe for the first time in public!

PUTTING YOURSELF IN THE PICTURE

Challenge group members to take time in the coming week to use part or all of this application section as an opportunity for continued growth.

LIVING EXCELLENT MORAL LIVES

PSALM 73

INTRODUCTION

We live in a world where moral compromise is rampant. Many things that were seen as morally questionable years ago are now standard operating procedure. But God calls us to moral excellence, no matter what anybody else does or says.

Too many people are walking each day on the slippery stones of morally wrong behavior. They feel that they are getting away with something. Often it seems like they are. But God's Word is clear that no one gets away with sin. Psalm 73 shows us that sinful, rebellious lives always end badly . . . unless Jesus redeems them.

THE BIG PICTURE

Take time to read this introduction with the group. There are suggestions for how this can be done in the beginning of the leader's section.

A WIDE ANGLE VIEW

Question One We know it's true that we can follow Jesus, do the right things, seek moral excellence, and still end up struggling. We also can look around and see people who seem to rebel openly against God, yet their lives appear to be great. Take time as a group to reflect on this phenomenon. As you do, it will get you into the spirit of the first half of Psalm 73.

A BIBLICAL PORTRAIT

Read Psalm 73

Question Two The writer of Psalm 73 struggles deeply with this issue of the wicked prospering and the righteous struggling. He pours his heart out as he agonizes over what appears to be a radical injustice. Those who live morally questionable lives seem safe, secure, and prosperous. Those who are seeking moral excellence (in particular the writer of the psalm) feel plagued, punished, and hurting. It comes to the point that the psalmist wonders if it is even worth seeking God and trying to do right.

Then, everything changes when the psalmist enters the sanctuary of God in worship. Like a light switch going on, he sees everything clearly.

Question Three In the presence of God, the psalmist has his eyes opened. He sees the slippery rocks on which the wicked are walking. He sees their end. He realizes that evil does not win. He comes to understand that those who follow God are really the ones who win ... in the end.

No matter what our eyes might see in this world, God is still on the throne. At the end of the day, it is always right to seek moral excellence ... even when it might not seem to "pay off" immediately.

The sobering reality taught in the second half of Psalm 73 should also stir followers of Jesus to reach out to those who are living with moral compromise. When we see people walking on slippery stones, and even prospering, we should not envy them. Instead we should pity them and reach out with God's love. They are not getting away with anything. They will fall in this life, or crash in eternity. The love of God should compel us to speak truth to these people and invite them to Jesus, the only One who can heal their broken lives.

SHARPENING THE FOCUS

Read Snapshot "The Slippery Rock Principle" before Questions 4 & 5

Question Four Years ago I watched the rise of a superstar pastor who built a tremendous church, wrote books, had a radio program, and was a sought-after conference speaker.

Then one day I read in the newspaper that he had experienced a moral failure. His church was devastated, his wife left him, and his family was heartbroken. Many months later, when I happened to be speaking in his town, that pastor called me to ask if I would have breakfast with him.

As we sat across from each other in the hotel restaurant, he told me his story: "When I started traveling a lot, I was alone in hotel rooms. I could watch CNN, or I could watch some other things, or I could watch the cable stuff that I knew was morally wrong. I thought I could handle it," he said. "Then after a while I saw those advertisements that say you can talk to certain people on the telephone and have sexually explicit conversations." He said, "I thought I could handle that."

He described how he went from one slippery rock to the next and to the next. Then he told how he fell and what it was like to come home to his wife and children after he had been exposed. By the time he had finished, he was crying so hard his shoulders were heaving.

If this humbled pastor could talk to each of us, if the writer of Psalm 73 were to stand in front of us, they would both speak in perfect unison, "Get off slippery rocks right this moment! This day! Don't take one more step! You think you can get away with it. You think you can handle the next one. You can't ... you won't. Run for the moral high ground." These words would echo the heart of God. He is ready to forgive, heal, and help us. But we need to repent and run to Him.

Question Five In His grace, God is always sending warnings to His children. They come in many shapes and forms. Here are just some of the ways God calls us to turn from moral compromise and seek the high ground of His love: (1) through reading His Word, (2) by the voice of His Spirit, (3) as we hear sermons preached, (4) through the words of people who care about us, (5) by seeing examples of those who fall, (6) by getting caught, (7) by closing doors.

Read Snapshot "Return to the Moral High Ground" before Question 6

Question Six The next two questions are very vulnerable. Some group members won't be ready to talk at this deep of a level. But when we can admit where we have struggled in the past and even confess where we are struggling today, we bring issues into the light. In the spiritual world (when it comes to sin), when we keep it hidden in the dark, it grows. But, when we expose it to the light, sin dies. James writes:

Therefore confess your sins to each other and pray for each other so that you may be healed. The prayer of a righteous man is powerful and effective. (5:16)

There is power in confession. Invite your group members to enter a new level of vulnerability, prayer, and accountability. This might also be a good time to reinforce the importance of confidentiality in a small group. If people share deeply and their trust is betrayed, it can destroy a group.

NOTE: It may be wise to ask members to pair off or get in groups of three for these questions. Members often feel safer with one or two others they trust and may not yet feel that way in a group of eight to ten people. The key is having someone to talk to in confidence. This may need to occur at a time other than the meeting.

Read Snapshot "The Final Destination Principle" before Question 8

Question Eight In the past Christians often spoke of heaven and hell as motivators; however, more recently we tend to avoid such talk. The truth is, heaven is a powerful incentive. We don't follow Jesus just to get to heaven. But it is a glorious hope and promise. We don't reach out to people just so they avoid hell. What we want is for them to have a living relationship with Jesus.

PUTTING YOURSELF IN THE PICTURE

Challenge group members to take time in the coming week to use part or all of this application section as an opportunity for continued growth.

LIVING EXCELLENT RELATIONAL LIVES

ACTS 2:42–47;
1 JOHN 4:11–12;
JAMES 5:13–16

INTRODUCTION

A number of years ago I did a personal survey of some people at Willow Creek Church. I asked, "So what does your small group give you that you can't get at a weekend service?" As I listened I was amazed at how articulate people were. They loved the services and felt they were connecting with God as we worshiped together. They had deep appreciation for the sense of community we have as a whole church. But all kinds of things were happening in small groups that were not happening in gathered worship.

At first this bothered me. I found myself trying to figure out how to make the worship services function in a way that could take people to deeper places of growth, connection, accountability, and life. Then it hit me. If we are going to live excellent lives, followers of Jesus need corporate worship *and* small group connections. It is not an either/or proposition, but both/and. There is a certain work God does in us when we are in large gatherings and another kind of ministry of the Holy Spirit that comes when we are in small groups.

This session is about celebrating some of the values and benefits of small groups. Since you are in a small group already, this should be affirming. As your group looks at five different values of small groups, pray that your group might go deeper in each of these areas. Pray also that the members of your group will live more excellent relational lives because they are part of your small group.

THE BIG PICTURE

Take time to read this introduction with the group. There are suggestions for how this can be done in the beginning of the leader's section.

A Wide Angle View

Question One Human beings were made by a God who is a community of persons. Biblical Christianity is different from every other major world religion, each which has a "god" who is a singular personage. In biblical Christianity, three distinct persons—the Father, the Son, and the Holy Spirit—make up the Godhead. Called the Trinity, they have enjoyed community in the Godhead from eternity past to eternity future.

When it came to creation, God the Father stepped to the forefront, but the Son and the Spirit were involved as well. When it came to redemption, the Son went to the forefront by dying on the cross. But the Father and the Spirit were actively engaged in this work. The Holy Spirit takes the forefront when it comes to growing people into Christlikeness. But the Father and the Son are working here also. There's mutuality and relationship that exists eternally in the Godhead.

We were made in God's image, and this means we are hardwired for community. God invites us into a quality of community that's beyond anything we could imagine. We are made for deep relational connection with God and with each other. This is one of the reasons that we need to be in small clusters of believers, in a setting where we can connect on a more significant and enduring level. There are things God wants to do in us and through us that will only happen when we live in close proximity to other believers.

A Biblical Portrait

Read Acts 2:42–47; 1 John 4:11–12; and James 5:13–16

Question Two As these passages illustrate, an extensive list of both practices (behaviors) and attitudes marked the first-century church's DNA. Identify these characteristics and then grapple with how we are doing at emulating them in the church today.

Sharpening the Focus

Read Snapshot "Love and Affirmation " before Question 4

Question Four Look at the general topic of how love and affirmation can be expressed in a small group. But be sure to "take this home" to your group. Pray that this will be a natural time to go deeper in how your group expresses love to each other.

Read Snapshot "Life Application" before Question 5

Question Five If your small group members are from the same church, you might want to discuss the past weekend's service. What did you learn? How did it speak to you? What application have you felt prompted to make? Create space for mutual sharing and see if your group members' life applications go deeper as they learn from each other.

If your group members are from different churches, it could be fun for each one to give a short synopsis of the message they heard and how it impacted them; group members might discover some area of growth and life application they can glean from each other.

Read Snapshot "Accountability" before Question 6

Question Six As the group leader, seek to discern if people are ready to go one step deeper. If you feel they are open to it, ask if anyone would like your small group members to keep them accountable in a specific area of life. Leave space for group members to tell about an area they are seeking to grow, develop a discipline, or stop a behavior pattern. After they tell about their area of desired growth, clarify how group members can best keep them accountable. Then pray for them as a group and promise to follow up.

Read Snapshot "Major Life Decision" before Question 7

Question Seven This question could lead to a very long discussion. If your group works with tight time parameters, be sensitive to this. If several members are in the midst of processing major life decisions, you might want to devote your next gathering just to listening and processing these together as a group.

Read Snapshot "Confession" before Question 8

Question Eight If your group has a high level of confidentiality and trust, you might want to open some space for people to confess something that is on their heart. If people do, be ready to listen, minister, and offer support. If no one is ready to go this deep, don't feel bad. This will come with time.

PUTTING YOURSELF IN THE PICTURE

Challenge group members to take time in the coming week to use part or all of this application section as an opportunity for continued growth.

LIVING EXCELLENT FINANCIAL LIVES

MALACHI 3:6—12; PROVERBS 3:9—10

INTRODUCTION

This session focuses on how to live excellent financial lives. From the Old Testament to the New, there is plenty of teaching on how God wants us to view and use resources. In this session we will focus on one specific area of our financial lives … giving. In particular, we will dig into the biblical teaching on tithing, God's call for His people to give the first 10 percent of all they earn back to Him.

The Bible teaches that tithing is a starting point, a launching pad for all other financial concerns. If we don't get this one right, we are robbing and dishonoring God—and it will be difficult to live an excellent financial life.

If you have not yet entered into a life of joyful tithing, don't let this impact your leadership of this session. Let your preparation and study become an opportunity for God to speak to you. Invite the truth of God's Word to challenge you and shape your financial life.

THE BIG PICTURE

Take time to read this introduction with the group. There are suggestions for how this can be done in the beginning of the leader's section.

A WIDE ANGLE VIEW

Question One In Malachi's day the financial standards of excellence had plummeted. Almost everyone had their reasons for giving less than the full 10 percent of their earnings to God and His work—and they were quite brazen about it. Into this setting entered God's spokesperson, Malachi. He had no fear of the people's disapproval. He came to speak God's words, to reset the bar.

Malachi asked, "How do you folks feel about getting robbed? Pretty bad? Well, you should, it's a terrible thing. You would never rob anybody, would you? Would you ever rob your neighbor or your friend?"

The people answered, "No, we're incapable of doing such a thing. We would never rob anybody."

At that point, Malachi sprang the trap and said, "That's true. You probably don't take what's not yours from your neighbors and friends. So why in the world would you rob the God that you say you love and serve? If you have the common decency to not rob neighbors and friends, what would possess you to rob God of what He asks you to give Him? Every time you bring less than the full 10 percent of your earnings to God, you're ripping off the One who gave His very best for you. That's unthinkable and it's got to stop."

Imagine this modern-day scenario: You went out and built a company and grew it to great profitability. You also have five kids whom you've fed, clothed, educated, and provided for their whole life. Eventually they ask, "Mom, Dad, would you invite us into the family business? We know you've worked all your lives to prepare this successful company, so we'd like to be part of it." And, of course, you gladly say yes.

Now imagine ten years have passed, the kids are all still working for your company, but it is no longer profitable. In fact, it is going to have to shut down. Too late you discover that your kids have been embezzling and bleeding cash out from the company into their personal bank accounts the entire time.

How do you feel as a parent? You have been robbed by your own flesh and blood! Can you imagine a deeper hurt?

Here's the gist of what Malachi is saying to the people of his day, "This is not an impersonal accounting issue we're talking about. You're God's kids. He's your heavenly Father. All He's ever done is give and give and give. All He asks is that you take a tenth of that and return it to Him as a worship offering."

A BIBLICAL PORTRAIT

Read Malachi 3:6 – 12 and Proverbs 3:9 – 10

Question Two The book of Malachi has many sections that are written like a conversation between God and His people. Malachi 3:6 – 12 is one of those passages. As you read it, take note of the voices. Sometimes God speaks and sometimes the people respond. At times Malachi expresses what the people are thinking.

This passage has a clear focus on financial excellence. The prophet opens the discussion by talking about a very unusual victim of thievery. It's as though Malachi asks the people to get the conversation going, "Who's the last person on planet Earth, the last person in the universe you would expect to get robbed?" The answer, of course, is God. Then Malachi goes on to explain to the people that they are robbing God.

He wants them to realize that refraining from giving a tithe is a form of stealing ... from God. The other side of the coin is important also. If they will commit to tithe, if they will take this test and pass it, God promises blessings beyond what they can imagine.

Question Three Hundreds of years prior to Malachi, God had spelled out for people how they ought to handle their money excellently. God said: "Earn money ethically — no schemes, no corruption, no back-door deals, no gray areas." God also said: "Spend money wisely, not foolishly or carelessly; avoid destructive debt; save money consistently for your future; give money generously to the poor."

As a part of these overall financial guidelines, God established the practice of tithing. The word simply means a tenth; 10 percent. People would bring 10 percent of their earnings to their worship place as a symbol of gratefulness to God for His material blessings. The money was also to be used for supporting the ministry of their worshiping community.

If the people would follow these directives, God promised to bless them. This promise took various shapes and forms. God would open the floodgates of heaven and let good things rain down; He would protect their work and secure their income (preventing pests from destroying their crops); He would see that the other nations would look favorably on them. All of these pictures assured the people that committing to give God their first fruits would be worth it all.

SHARPENING THE FOCUS

Read Snapshot "The Heart Check" before Question 4

Question Four When someone lays down their life for you, when they wipe clean the slate of all your sins, when they invite you into their family, when they secure your eternity, and promise to bless your life today, how can you not joyfully give back to them?

When our heart grasps the love of God and His goodness toward us, our immediate response ought to be, "Yes, Lord! Whatever You want! Just say the word!"

If Malachi stood before us today, he'd say, "I don't care what you think of me. I don't care what the opinion polls are saying about me and my prophetic ministry." Malachi's concern was not about himself . . . it was about the glory of God.

If Malachi could preach his message today it might go something like this, "It is time to do a heart check. How do you look at a bloodstained cross and an empty tomb and not respond with generosity? How do you look at a rock-solid promise of a home in heaven forever and then quibble over giving 10 percent to the One who made it possible for you to live with this hope?"

Jesus said, "No one can serve two masters. One will always win — God or money." Malachi's question today is the same as it was thousands of years ago. Make sure God is first in your life, never money. One way to do this and live with financial excellence is to give the tithe to God.

Read Snapshot "The Gut Check" before Questions 6 & 7

Question Six If we don't take the time to build systems into our personal money management practices that make tithing automatic, we just might wind up looking back five years from now aching over the fact that we never got around to doing what God called us to do. This is why it is so important to do a gut check. This demands a level of character that gets real honest with God and self. It means putting systems in place that help us live in a way that honors God on a regular basis.

When Proverbs 3:9 calls us to honor the Lord with our first fruits, the idea is taken from an agricultural metaphor. When farmers wanted to bring a tithe of their harvest to God, they discovered that they ought to bring the very first of the harvest. If they did not bring the first 10 percent, sometimes there was nothing to give.

In our gut check we need to learn to give God the first 10 percent of what we earn. If we wait to give Him the last 10 percent, we might discover that it is all gone! By giving the first fruits, we can be sure that God always gets what He asks of us.

Question Seven As a leader, encourage each person to use the designated time for personal reflection and prayer. Even those who tithe will do well to think through how they are giving. Those who do not tithe might just hear from God in a new and fresh way that will set them free as they learn to give with joy-filled and generous hearts.

Read Snapshot "The Faith Check" before Question 8

Question Eight It really takes faith to honor God with our money. Every time we place money in an offering plate or give with a generous heart, we declare that we trust God to provide for us. In a world that is growing increasingly stingy, believers give a witness to God, to heaven, and to the world when we acknowledge that all we have is a gift from God. As we give, we declare our faith, and we grow our faith.

PUTTING YOURSELF IN THE PICTURE

Challenge group members to take time in the coming week to use part or all of this application section as an opportunity for continued growth.

LIVING EXCELLENT DIRECTIONAL LIVES

JAMES 1:5–8; PSALM 119:105; ROMANS 8:14; PROVERBS 11:14; COLOSSIANS 4:3

INTRODUCTION

We don't have to wander through life with no direction. We also do not have to figure out everything on our own. God is ready to give us direction if we ask for it with faith and follow His leading.

God offers direction to His children in various ways. In this study we will look at four of them: the teaching of the Bible, promptings of the Holy Spirit, the wisdom of godly people, and circumstances. If we seek God's wisdom, He is ready and willing to give it.

THE BIG PICTURE

Take time to read this introduction with the group. There are suggestions for how this can be done in the beginning of the leader's section.

A WIDE ANGLE VIEW

Question One Every follower of Jesus knows what it is to listen for God's direction, and then to follow it. And all of us have experienced moments when we fail to seek God's directional wisdom and do things on our own. As you begin this session, pray for honest vulnerability as group members share their stories of success and failure in this area of directional excellence.

A Biblical Portrait

Read James 1:5–8; Psalm 119:105; Romans 8:14; Proverbs 11:14; and Colossians 4:3

Question Two This assortment of passages addresses a number of the ways God speaks to His children. For instance, in Psalm 119:105 we learn that God's Word gives us direction as it shines light on our path. In Proverbs 11:14 we read how God brings wisdom through the counsel of other people. In Colossians 4:3 we read about the apostle Paul asking for an "open door for the message," a clear example of God using circumstances to direct His people.

Sharpening the Focus

Read Snapshot "Faith Instead of Doubt" before Question 3

Question Three Every moment of every day we are inundated with worldly "wisdom," all sorts of voices offering us direction for our lives. But God calls us to ask *Him* for wisdom and believe He is ready to give it. We are not to doubt this truth but to be confident of it.

Read Snapshot "Biblical Direction" before Question 4

Question Four Do you need to learn how to handle money, treat your body, or deal with an anger problem? Are you struggling with anxiety, fear, or guilt? Do you want to know how to build a strong marriage? Are you looking for the basics of parenting? Do you need to repair a broken relationship? God's Word offers clear, practical teaching on all of these issues and so much more!

Do you need to know how your sins can be washed away and how you can go to heaven when you die? The Bible offers straightforward information about how God forgives guilty sinners through Christ's sacrificial death on the cross.

From practical life issues, such as how to handle business finances, to deeply spiritual topics, such as freedom from guilt, the Bible gives excellent directional teaching. If we read God's Word, learn it, and follow it, many of life's questions will be answered.

Read Snapshot "Holy Spirit Promptings" before Question 6

Question Six One way God guides His people is somewhat subjective. It takes a while to grow spiritually to the point where we become knowledgeable about how Holy Spirit promptings work. We cannot discount them or say they're not important. In John 10 Jesus says that the sheep recognize the voice of the shepherd. As God's sheep, we need to learn to recognize when the Spirit is speaking to us. When He says, "stop," we need to freeze in our tracks. When he says, "Go," "Give," "Serve," "Proclaim My grace," or anything else, we need to be ready to respond.

A quick qualifier here ... God's leadings, the Spirit's promptings, always are consistent with the teaching of His written Word. God's Spirit, the third person of the Trinity, will never ask us to do anything that violates Scripture.

Read Snapshot "Other People" before Question 7

Question Seven In His grace, God places wise people in our lives. Typically they are more mature believers who have traveled many years and miles with Jesus. God will often speak through these men and women, if we are willing to listen. We ought to identify several such people and seek their input and perspective on a regular basis. Again, we must test their insights against Scripture and use discernment. But we can gain a great deal of helpful direction from individuals and groups who offer godly counsel.

Read Snapshot "Circumstances" before Question 9

Question Nine The apostle Paul talked about how God opens doors and closes doors. As we seek direction in our lives, sensitivity to God's movement in circumstances is very helpful. But it is important to remember that we are not called to walk through every open door. In the same way, a closed door does not necessarily mean God is saying no. These circumstances give some insight, but we must then pray, seek the insight of Scripture, be sensitive to any prompting from the Holy Spirit, and gain wisdom from others.

PUTTING YOURSELF IN THE PICTURE

Challenge group members to take time in the coming week to use part or all of this application section as an opportunity for continued growth.

LIVING EXCELLENT ETERNAL LIVES

JOHN 1:12 – 13;
EPHESIANS 2:8 – 9;
TITUS 3:4 – 7

INTRODUCTION

We have looked at how to live excellent lives over the past five sessions. In this closing study we focus on eternity. Jesus asked the question, "What good is it for a man to gain the whole world, yet forfeit his soul?" (Mark 8:36). No matter how good this life might be for someone, it is a snap of a finger compared to eternity. God wants us to seek excellence in this life, but He also longs for us to experience an excellent eternity.

Such assurance comes when we know and embrace Jesus Christ. Heaven is a gift of grace, but it must be received. Those who are followers of Jesus will rejoice to reflect on all that awaits them as forgiven children of God. Those who have not yet accepted the forgiveness and new life that are offered by Jesus will learn about the amazing hope of heaven. If you have any group members who are not yet followers of Jesus, pray for the Holy Spirit to use this session to draw them to the Savior.

THE BIG PICTURE

Take time to read this introduction with the group. There are suggestions for how this can be done in the beginning of the leader's section.

A WIDE ANGLE VIEW

Question One Some people come to realize the brevity of life as a young girl or boy when a parent, grandparent, or friend passes away. Others travel farther down life's road before an illness or serious injury awakens them to this sobering truth. This conversation might be light or it could become very heavy if people share about losing loved ones.

A BIBLICAL PORTRAIT

Read Ephesians 2:8–9 and Titus 3:4–7 before Question 2

Question Two Is salvation based on what I do or what Jesus has done? That is the big question. In these passages, over and over again, it is articulated with bold clarity that salvation is based on the work of Jesus Christ. His life, His death, His resurrection, His grace, and His love are the bedrock of our salvation. We could never earn or deserve what He offers freely. Yes, we need to receive the gift, but it is exactly that, a gift of grace (Eph. 2:8–9). As followers of Jesus we would do well to meditate on these passages and remember, on a daily basis, that many things in this life have to be earned and deserved, but the grace of God is not one of them.

Read John 14:6; Acts 4:11–12; Romans 10:9–10; and John 1:12–13 before Question 3

Question Three The story of Jesus is a journey of grace. From beginning to end, the road to heaven has signs that all point to Jesus. He left the glory of heaven to come and show us the way home (Phil. 2:5–8). He goes ahead of us to prepare a place (John 14:2–3). His death pays the price for our entry to heaven (Col. 1:20). And His resurrection assures us that we too can spend eternity in glory (1 Cor. 15). The one and only way a sinful person can find cleansing from sin and live with assurance that heaven will be their home for eternity is through faith in Jesus Christ.

SHARPENING THE FOCUS

Read Snapshot "A Glorious and Undeserved Gift" before Question 4

Question Four In a world where many people seek to earn God's love, the Scriptures teach something that is radically counterintuitive. God loves us before we do anything (John 3:16). He sent Jesus to pay the price for our wrongs when we were still rebellious and filthy with sin (Rom. 5:8). No one deserves grace. Forgiveness can never be earned. It is a gift.

Somewhere along the way in our spiritual journey toward Jesus, this sinks in. We come to the personal awareness that God loves us beyond description and reason. The Father gave His beloved Son for us, even though we deserved judgment and death. This is the good news of the gospel.

When this truth grips our heart, everything changes. We worship with passion and joy. We want others to know this life-changing love. When we sin, we run to God instead of hiding because we know He already sees our sin and has dealt with it. When we encounter people who are still far from God and perhaps living in open rebellion, we are not offended or repulsed. Instead, we recognize that we were once just like them and we seek to point them toward the Savior who changed our life.

Read Snapshot "The Way to Heaven" before Question 6

Question Six *Pluralism* is the belief that many religions lead to God. *Universalism* is the belief that everyone will go to heaven. Both of these philosophies are growing in popularity. The problem is, they do not reflect the teaching of Jesus or the Bible. Scripture is clear that the only way to heaven is through a living, faith-filled relationship with Jesus. No matter how popular a philosophy might become, Christians know that the teaching of the Bible is our only source of truth.

Read Snapshot "The Glory of Heaven" before Question 9

Question Nine These images and pictures of heaven should fill us with anticipation and hope.

PUTTING YOURSELF IN THE PICTURE

Challenge group members to take time in the coming week to use part or all of this application section as an opportunity for continued growth.

WILLOW
Willow Creek Resources

Willow Creek Association
Vision, Training, Resources for Prevailing Churches

This resource was created to serve you and to help you build a local church that prevails. It is just one of many ministry tools published by the Willow Creek Association.

The Willow Creek Association (WCA) was created in 1992 to serve a rapidly growing number of churches from across the denominational spectrum that are committed to helping unchurched people become fully devoted followers of Christ. Membership in the WCA now numbers over 12,000 Member Churches worldwide from more than ninety denominations.

The Willow Creek Association links like-minded Christian leaders with each other and with strategic vision, training and resources in order to help them build prevailing churches designed to reach their redemptive potential.

For specific information about WCA conferences, resources, membership and other ministry services contact:

Willow Creek Association
P.O. Box 3188
Barrington, IL 60011-3188
Phone: 847.570.9812
Fax: 847.765.5046
www.willowcreek.com

Interactions Series

Big Questions

Clear Answers to Confusing Issues

Bill Hybels with Kevin and Sherry Harney

A PERSPECTIVE LIKE NO OTHER

Life is filled with big questions, and it seems everyone has a different answer. Whether from pop culture, political figures, conventional wisdom, or our friends, we are inundated with conflicting advice and opinions. Where can we go to find clear answers to the confusing issues we face?

God is ready to give us the wisdom and insight needed to navigate the questions that seem too big for us:

- Will wars ever cease?
- Can our planet survive?
- How do I balance life's demands?
- Is God really out there?
- Does God hear my prayers?
- Aren't all religions the same?

Answers to these questions are not simple. Only God has the vantage point needed to help us. He has a perspective like no other. God made the universe and holds it in His hands. He alone can answer our toughest questions.

Softcover: 978-0-310-28065-1

Pick up a copy at your favorite bookstore!

ZONDERVAN®
.com

Interactions Series

Celebrating God

Discover the Truth of God's Character

Bill Hybels with Kevin and Sherry Harney

ARE YOU READY TO CELEBRATE?

A stadium full of football fans jump to their feet and cheer with deafening volume when a game-winning pass is caught. Family members gather every year to give gifts and sing choruses of Happy Birthday. Friends congregate just to have a party ... they hardly need a reason. In the Bible God instituted festivals and feasts. There is something in the human spirit that loves to rejoice, shout, and celebrate ... and God likes it that way.

We were created for celebration, and the focal point of our praise should always be God. When we get glimpses of His character, expressions of joy should spontaneously erupt. God is a refuge; He is generous and righteous, full of extravagant love toward us. The Maker of heaven and earth is relational, He guides us, and He will never leave us. It's time to discover God's character and make Him the focal point of our celebration.

Softcover: 978-0-310-28063-7

Interactions Series

Influence

Maximizing Your Impact for God

Bill Hybels with Kevin and Sherry Harney

YOUR LIFE MEANS MORE THAN YOU KNOW

God wants you to be a world changer ... starting right where you are today. Your acts of service, words of truth, love for God, care for people, and all you do each day can have a transformational impact on the people around you. In a world filled with darkness and discouragement, the light of heaven can shine through you.

Jesus was the most influential person in human history. He brought joy to the sorrowful, hope to the broken, purpose to the wandering, and forgiveness to all who would receive Him. The ministry of Jesus continues today. One way the Savior brings His world-changing message to this generation is through you and me.

It's time for us to let the Holy Spirit flow freely. It's time to influence the world with the love of Jesus. It's time to maximize our impact for God!

Softcover: 978-0-310-28066-8

Pick up a copy at your favorite bookstore!

ReGroup™

Training Groups to Be Groups

Henry Cloud, Bill Donahue, and *John Townsend*

Whether you're a new or seasoned group leader, or whether your group is well-established or just getting started, the *ReGroup*™ small group DVD and participant's guide will lead you and your group together to a remarkable new closeness and effectiveness. Designed to foster healthy group interaction and facilitate maximum growth, this innovative approach equips both group leaders and members with essential skills and values for creating and sustaining truly life-changing small groups. Created by three group life experts, the two DVDs in this kit include:

- Four sixty-minute sessions on the foundations of small groups that include teaching by the authors, creative segments, and activities and discussion time
- Thirteen five-minute coaching segments on topics such as active listening, personal sharing, giving and receiving feedback, prayer, calling out the best in others, and more

A participant's guide is sold separately.

DVD: 978-0-310-27783-5
Participant's Guide: 978-0-310-27785-9

Pick up a copy at your favorite bookstore!

 ZONDERVAN®
.com

Share Your Thoughts

With the Author: Your comments will be forwarded to
the author when you send them to *zauthor@zondervan.com*.

With Zondervan: Submit your review of this book
by writing to *zreview@zondervan.com*.

Free Online Resources at
www.zondervan.com

Zondervan AuthorTracker: Be notified whenever your favorite
authors publish new books, go on tour, or post an update
about what's happening in their lives at www.zondervan.com/
authortracker.

Daily Bible Verses and Devotions: Enrich your life with daily
Bible verses or devotions that help you start every morning
focused on God. Visit www.zondervan.com/newsletters.

Free Email Publications: Sign up for newsletters on Christian
living, academic resources, church ministry, fiction, children's
resources, and more. Visit www.zondervan.com/newsletters.

Zondervan Bible Search: Find and compare Bible passages in
a variety of translations at www.zondervanbiblesearch.com.

Other Benefits: Register yourself to receive online benefits
like coupons and special offers, or to participate in research.

ZONDERVAN®

ZONDERVAN.com/
AUTHORTRACKER
follow your favorite authors